This book belongs to:

_____

THE ADVENTURES OF
TORAH AND ROBIN

Torah and Robin go to

AGRA

BARU & JEKA

TOR★H is a six-year-old girl whose mind is filled with wonder.

Her name means star and she is a star in her own eyes and in the eyes of her brother. Torah always sees adventure in everything and drags her big brother along into it.

Her elder brother, Robin is eight.

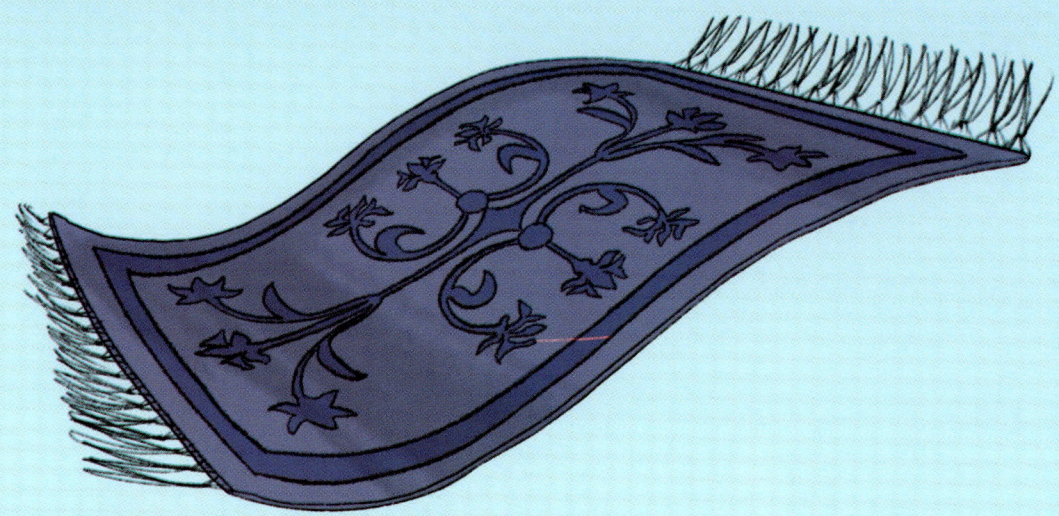

ROBIN

Robin loves his sister and her crazy ideas. If Torah is the star of her own little stories, then Robin is the smart, sharp detective who helps his sister solve mysteries and in doing that, helps people.

So Torah and Robin happily go along on adventures.

At 5am, while most children around the world are asleep, Torah and Robin are up and about.

They are packing their backpacks and Mummy helps them.

It's summer time, and today they are heading to Agra with Daddy.

He wants to buy a new carpet for their home. The old one is now tattered and falling apart.

This is a good chance for the children to see a new city and have lots of adventures.

They reach New Delhi Railway Station to catch a train to Agra.

It's a super fast train called the Shatabdi Express.

Torah adores train journeys. It's the sound of the wheels on the tracks that she enjoys the most.

Clackity clack, Clackity clack, Clackity clack!

The idea that they are going to a new place fills her with a tingling sense of excitement.

Toot!! Toot!! The train is off!

As the train leaves the city of Delhi behind, it rolls through beautiful green and gold fields full of crops that are ready to be harvested.

The children are staring out of the large picture window and counting every cow and buffalo they pass.

The children are served a hot breakfast. An omelette and toast for Torah because she loves to eat eggs and steaming hot Upma for Robin.

'Look!!! Is that a mummy deer and her family?' yells Torah, whose sharp eyes have once again spotted something strange in the fields.

'Those are not deer. Those are Neelgai, they are antelope. They are different from deer,' says Robin sagely!

'And how do you know that? They look just like deer to me,' says Torah with a huff.

Deer and antelope are different

↳ Antelopes have horns that are permanent and don't branch.

↳ Male deer have antlers that grow and fall every year and are branched.

'I have read about them in a book,' says Robin, who always has something to read with him.

Little pocket books about animals and trees, space, mountains and rivers are his favourite things in the world …

WHAT ARE YOUR 5 FAVOURITE THINGS IN THE WORLD?

1.
2.
3.
4.
5.

She wants to draw the beautiful fields and the deer family—no, the antelope family that she has just seen, before she forgets what they look like.

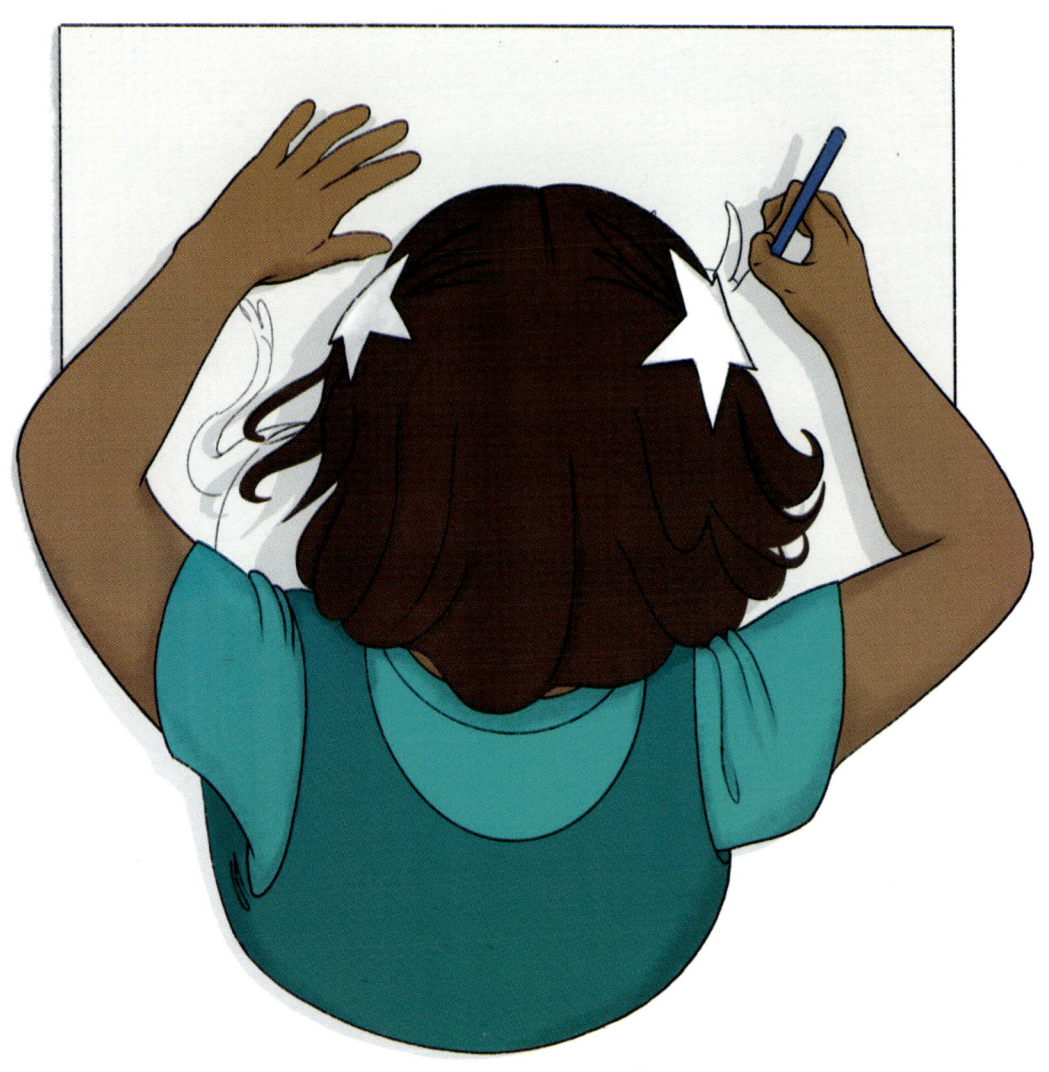

DRAW YOUR FAVOURITE ANIMAL HERE

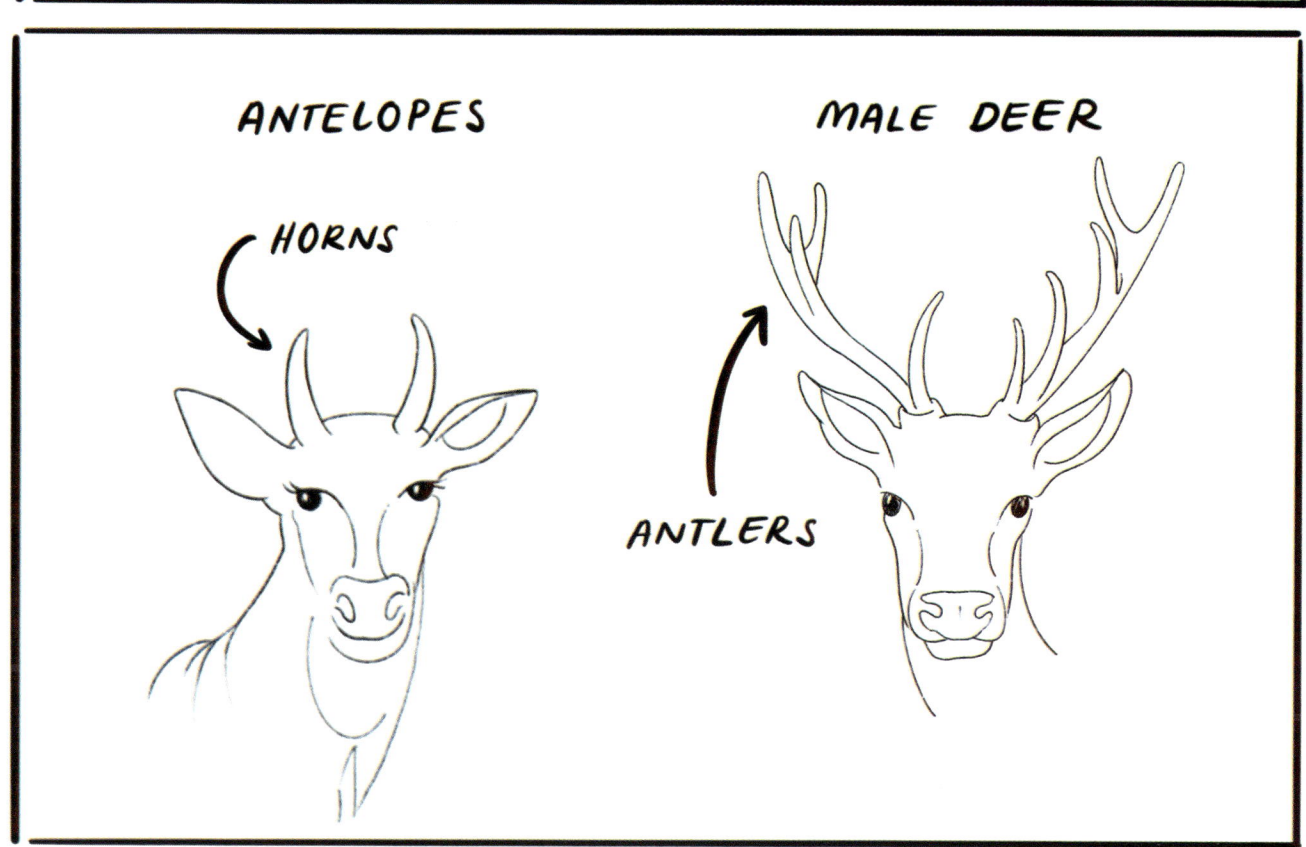

The train rolls into Agra Cantonment station and the family zips away to the carpet factory.

Mr David is waiting for them at the gate, he leads them into the brightly coloured building that looks like a large godown or warehouse.

'He reminds me of a Baby Hippo,' says Robin with a wink.
Torah says, *'That's just rude, Robin!'*
and starts giggling.

COMPANY

COTTON   WOOL   SILK

Mr David knows all about carpets and how they are made. He shows the children how carpets are made from cotton, wool and silk.

'Now, handmade carpets are made one knot at a time,' he says.

He shows them how a beautiful silk carpet takes months to make and how a carpet needs to be cleaned and cared for.

Mr David shows the children how
a carpet is cut and cleaned and made
ready to be sent off to the buyers.

The children are fascinated by it all and ask
a lot of questions...

'Was Aladdin's flying carpet made here in Agra?'
asks Torah, and this sets off Mr David into such a
huge burst of laughter that his belly does not stop
shaking for a full five minutes.

'*Our carpets are sent off to all corners of the world,*' says Mr David quite proudly.

In the meantime, their Daddy has found the carpet he was looking for, negotiated a good price and made the payment.

They are now free to have lunch and then go see the sights Agra has to offer.

They have lunch at a local restaurant inside Hotel Maya.

It's not a very pretty place but it is very clean.

Lunch is a special type of puri called **badai** that is made hot and fresh along with **sabzi** made with potatoes and tomatoes.

For dessert, children eat five hot jalebis each.

The children know that their Daddy always gets a guide.

'They know things that are not given in the books,' Robin says to his Daddy with a twinkle in his eye.

Mr Bhadra takes them through the huge gates and up the ramp to the palace of Emperor Akbar. The ramp is covered with dents and grooves and is not flat and smooth.

'This is to help the horses get a good foothold,' says Mr Bhadra.

Torah likes Emperor Akbar immediately because if a King can think for the good of his horses, then he is a good king.

It's the middle of the day by now and it's gotten quite hot.

The children keep having small sips of water from their water bottles whenever they feel thirsty.

The guide now brings them to a very big stone pot. It is huge!!

'This is the royal bath tub,' he announces.

'The bath tub is so big that a horse can have a swim in it,' says Torah and she and Robin make horsey sounds.

Neigh! Neigh!

Suddenly Torah says, '*LOOK There–over there!*'

She is pointing towards the Neem tree growing to the right of the courtyards.

'*It's a baby squirrel!*' she says.

Now we know that Torah has sharp eyes but just how she spotted the baby squirrel will remain a mystery to us.

Torah and Robin scramble over to the Neem tree and kneel down near the tiny creature.

'Oh! poor little squirrel,' says Torah, who is quite puzzled and does not know what to do.

'I think the little squirrel is thirsty and dehydrated because of the summer heat,' says Robin, solving the puzzle.

'It needs a few sips of water,' says Torah.

He whips out his bottle and drops a few beads of water into the squirrel's mouth. He drops some water on the rest of the squirrel as well to cool down the poor creature.

The effect is like a miracle!!

The squirrel begins to wriggle. It rubs its front legs over its head like only squirrels can, gives one look at the two children and shoots off up the Neem tree.

Once up the tree it turns once again to look at the children.

'It is saying, thank you, Robin,' says Torah.

'You are the one who spotted the little squirrel, thank you, Torah,' says Robin.

'If the emperor can have such a huge bath tub, surely he can leave a few small tubs of water for the birds and squirrels,' says Torah.

'I will certainly talk to the chief of the archaeology department,' says a fuddled Mr Bhadra.

The children were happy to hear that and now they are excited to go see the Taj Mahal.

TAJ MAHAL

'It is one of the seven wonders of the world,' says Mr Bhadra.

It is approaching sunset and the Taj Mahal is glowing with a golden light.

The children walk about as the guide explains many historic details about the beautiful building that was built by the Emperor Shah Jahan in the loving memory of his wife, Mumtaz Mahal.

'Do you know that the Taj looks pink in the morning light and glows orange in the evening,' says Mr Bhadra.

Colour this page
orange glow at sunset

PINK TINT AT SUNRISE

The gardens are beautiful and Torah can see many, many green parakeets flying about from tree to tree.

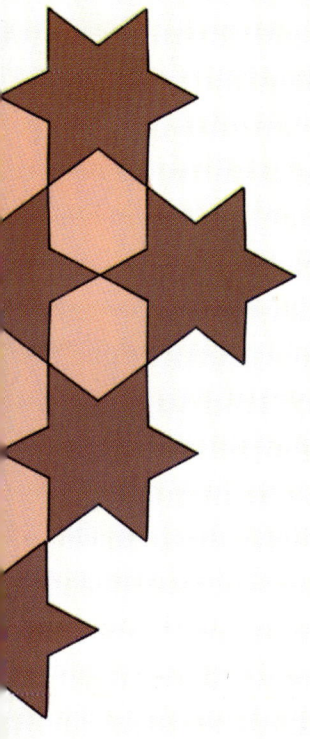

'This is an exact drawing of the moon and the star that are placed on the very top of the big dome of the Taj Mahal,' says Mr Bhadra. *'Look up there.'*

Torah looks up and then looks down again.

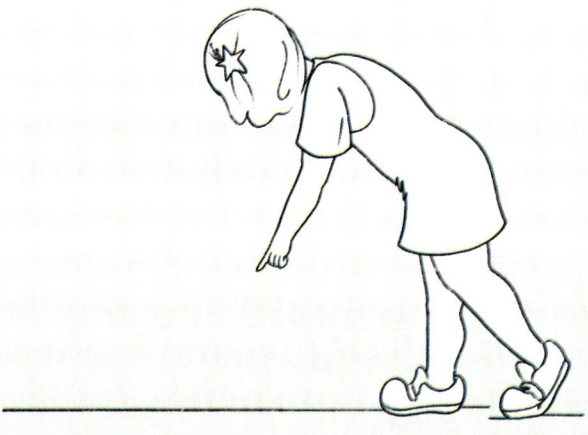

After looking up and down one more time, she says, *'The moon and star up there look so small and this looks so big!!'*

'That's because the top of the dome is far away, Torah,' says Robin.

'Like a plane looks small in the sky and big at the airport,' says Torah.

COLOUR THIS PAGE

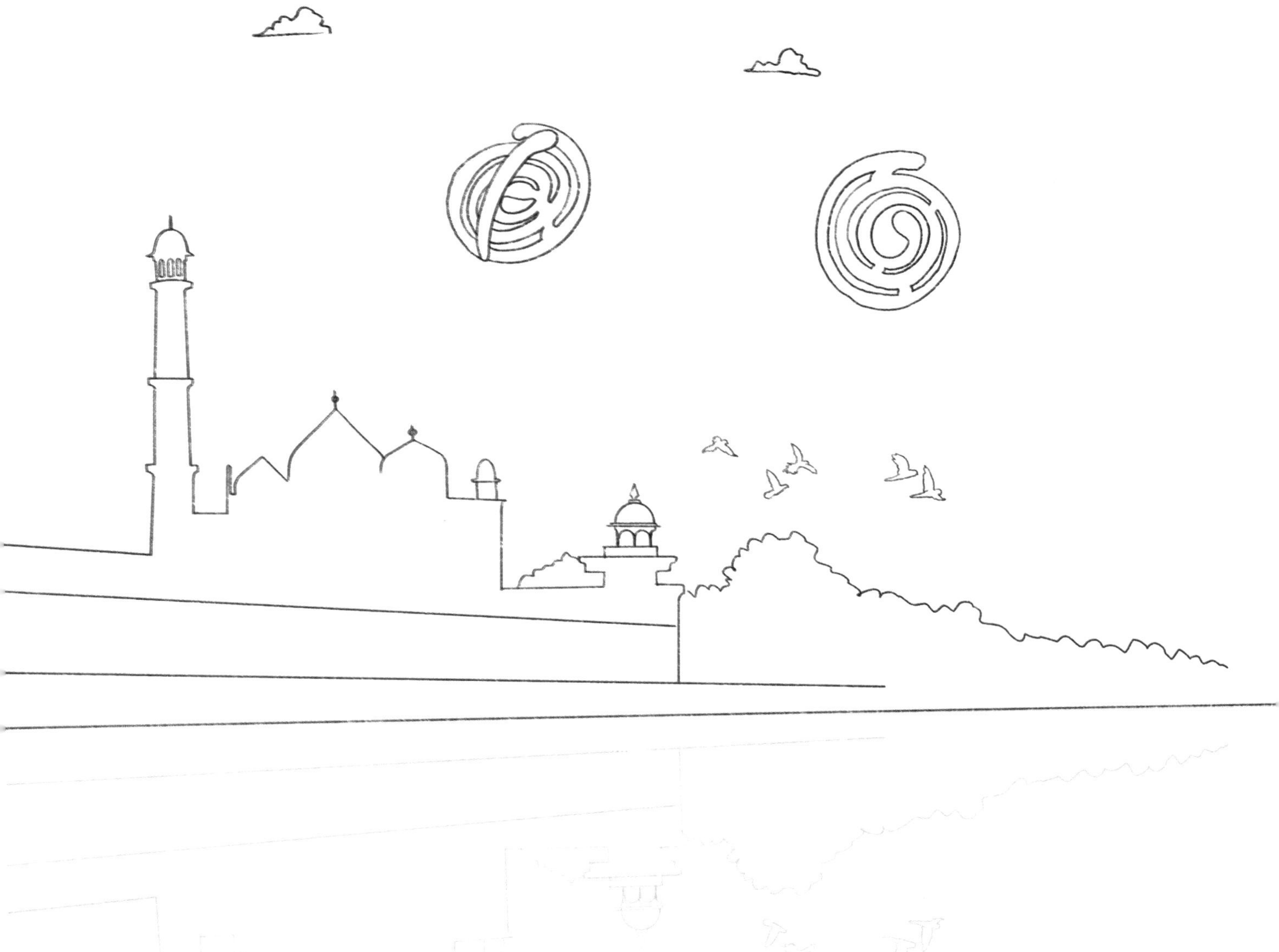

Torah and Robin are sad to leave Agra and on the train back, Torah draws the Yamuna river behind the Taj Mahal with squirrels and parakeets, while Robin thinks about carpets and jalebis.

YAMUNA RIVER

Later at night when the children are back home and have had a big dinner, they are sitting on the new carpet and talking about the day.

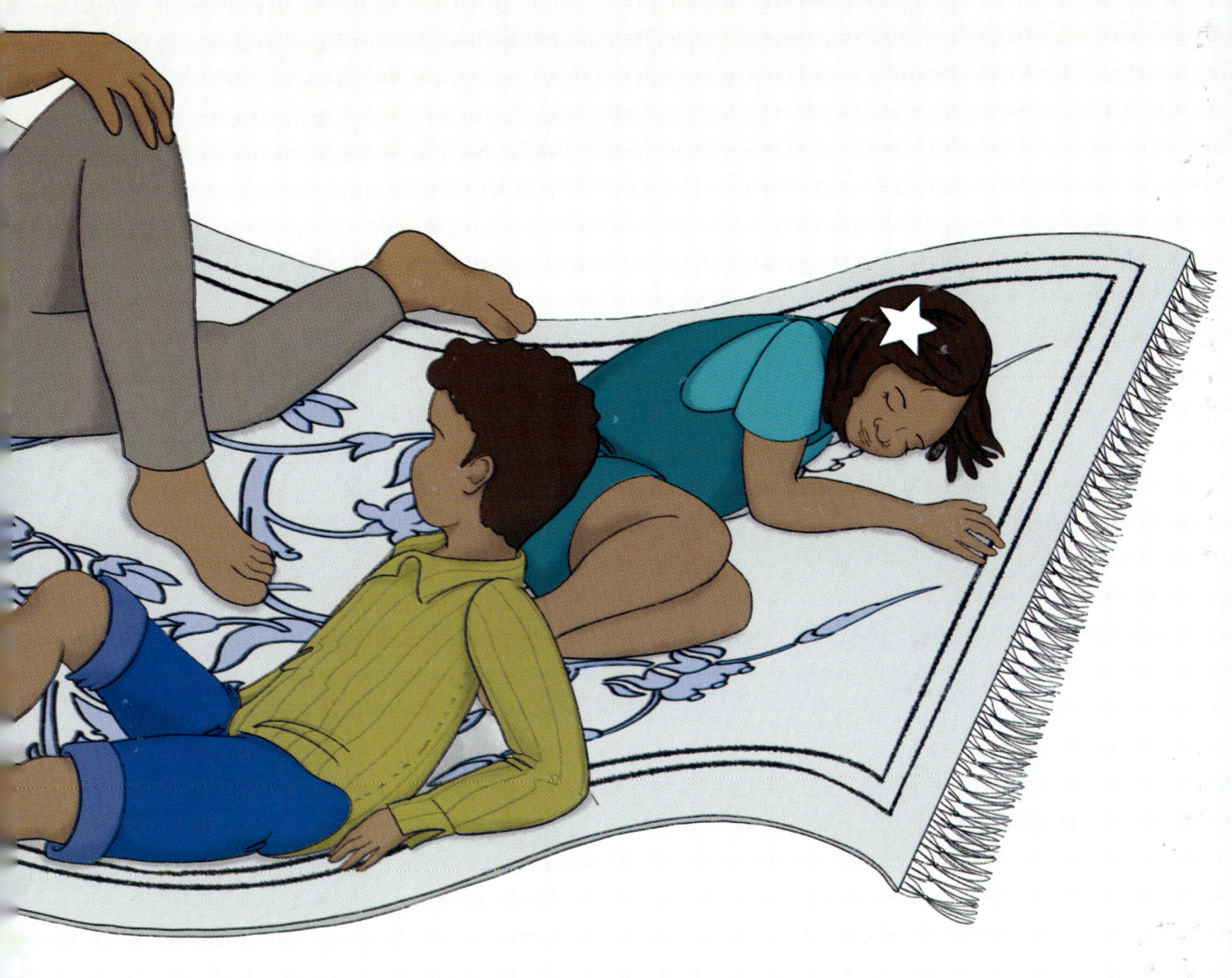

'Could this actually be Alladin's carpet? Do you think it can fly?' asks Robin.

'Of course it is Robin, and yes it can fly. All you have to do is lay down your head, close your eyes ...and DREAM,' says his mother as Robin drifts off to sleep.

Written by Rajesh Chandra Baruah

In the past, Baru has been a waiter, tour leader, raft guide, and film-maker. Now he is mostly a storyteller, home-stay owner, driver, cleaner, and cook. This is his second book.

Visualised by Jessica Rivas

Jeka is a coffee lover, dreamer, illustrator, and designer. She has travelled from her native Venezuela to Spain and from there to other parts of the world.

Jeka and Baru are friends.

We deeply thank our literary agent, Suhail Mathur, and his incredible team at The Book Bakers for guiding us through this journey. Our publisher Renu Kaul Verma and Vitasta Publishers, your support, expertise, and dedication have been instrumental in bringing our work to life.

Thank you for sharing this adventure with us.

With heartfelt appreciation,
Baru & Jeka